the comings and goings of

david beckham

david

the comings and goings of
beckham

D&C
David and Charles

london • 1999

plaza de oriente, madrid • september 2003

arriving at the 19 management birthday party, london • april 2004

arriving at the mtv movie awards, los angeles • may 2003

madrid • november 2003

arriving at upton park football ground, london • august 1998

in rio de janeiro • 2000

heathrow airport arrivals • july 1997

heathrow airport arrivals • june 1997

london • january 1999

leaving the sanderson hotel, london • june 2000

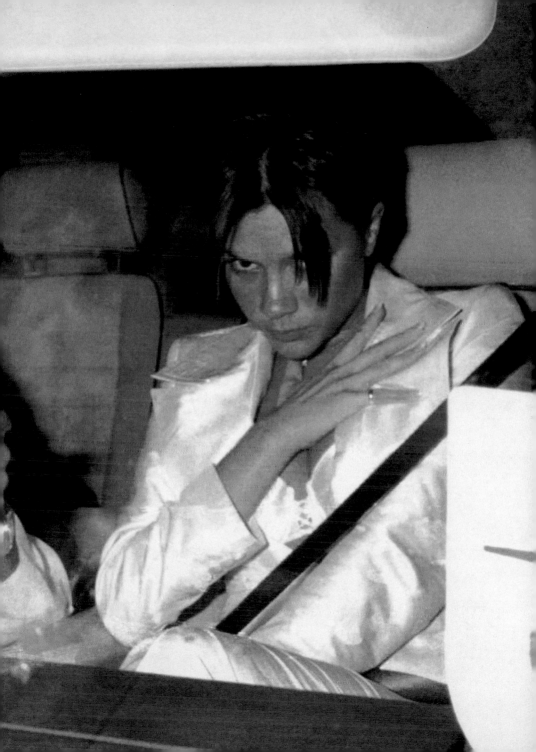

arriving for a meeting with damon dash, new york • may 2003

arriving at a press conference, madrid • july 2003

leaving for south africa, luton airport • may 2003

leaving following the christening of elizabeth hurley's son, london · uly 2002

leaving a filling station, madrid • april 2004

madrid · february 2004

arriving at a press conference, madrid • november 2003

arriving in majorca with real madrid • august 2003

arriving back in madrid after a tour of the far east • august 2003

at the wedding of davinia taylor and dave gardner, cheshire • july 2003

at the funeral of jimmy davis, worcestershire · august 2003

arriving at the versace jeans boutique party, london • 1999

canada · 1998

leaving the real madrid training ground · september 2004

leaving the ivy restaurant, london • 1999

leaving the down hall hotel, berkshire • march 1999

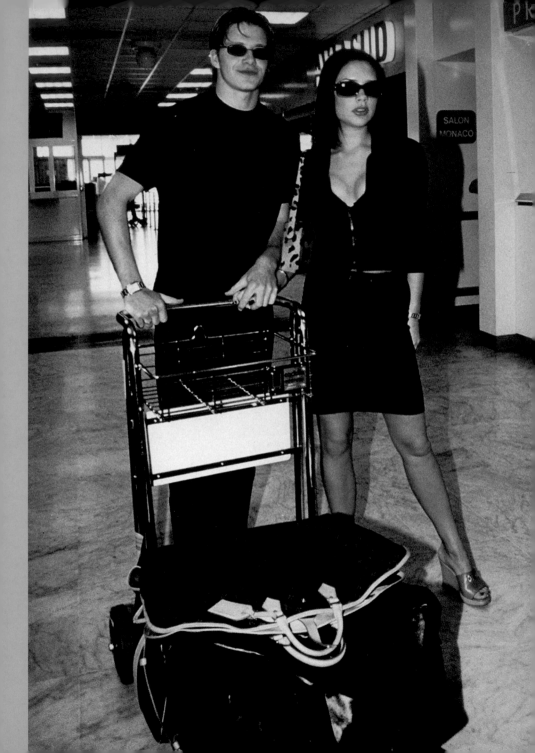

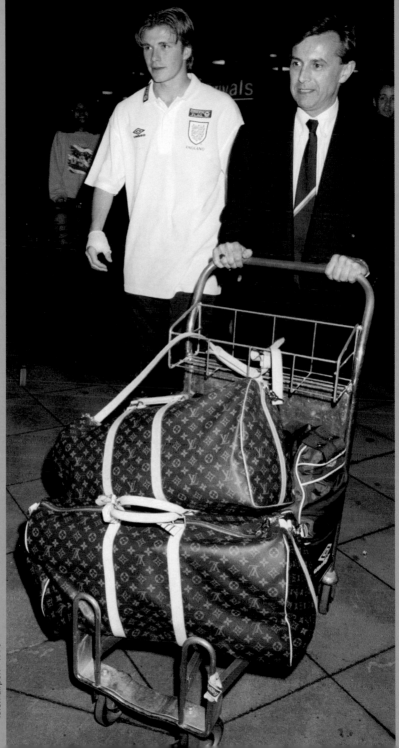

leaving the red cube bar, london • november 2000

leaving brown's nightclub, london • march 2000

leaving brondby training ground, copenhagen • july 1998

visiting tsukiji primary school, tokyo • january 2000

brooklyn's first birthday party, cottons hotel, cheshire • march 2000

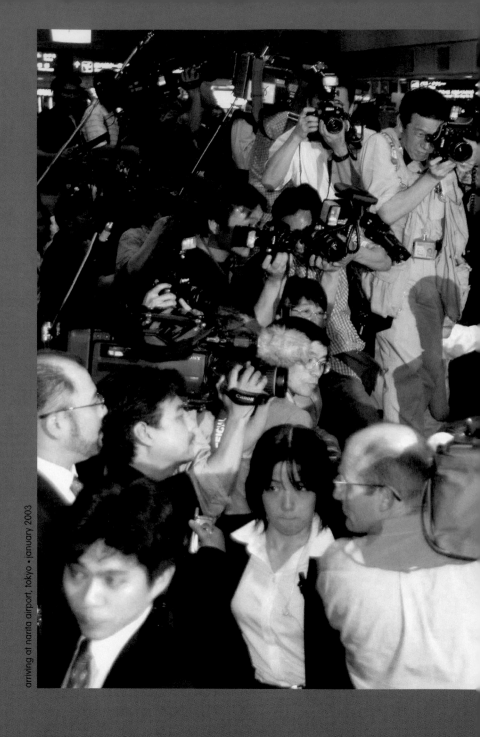

arriving at narita airport, tokyo • january 2003

heathrow airport arrivals • july 1999

'arriving back in mexico on the real madrid team coach after a tour of the far east' · august 2003

ESTEBAN RIVAS®

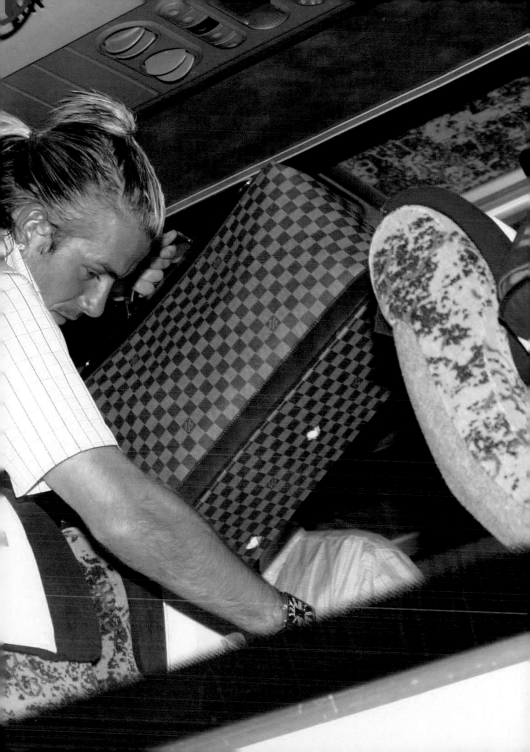

leaving a hotel near crewe • january 1998

leaving the 'party in the park' concert, london • july 2000

at jade jagger's party, st. martin's lane hotel, london • september 1999

leaving the down hall hotel, hertfordshire • march 1999

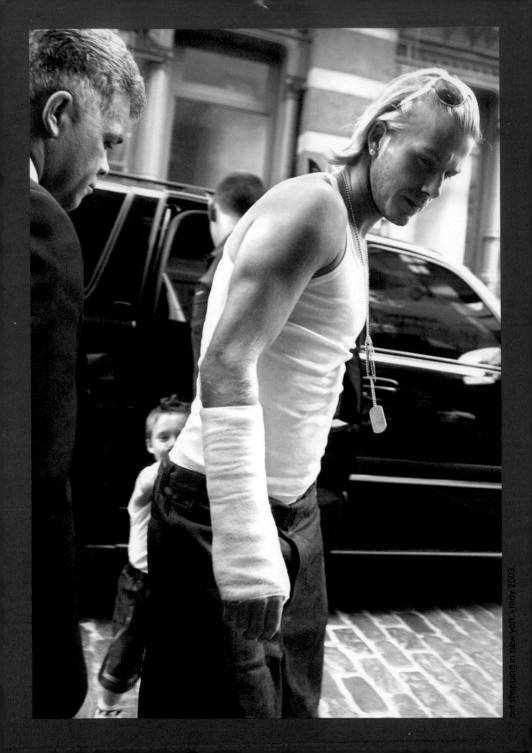

arriving at the café royal, london • june 1999

shopping in new york • may 2003

arriving at victoria's parents' house, hertfordshire • 1997

leaving a restaurant, madrid • april 2004

leaving the real madrid training ground · august 2004

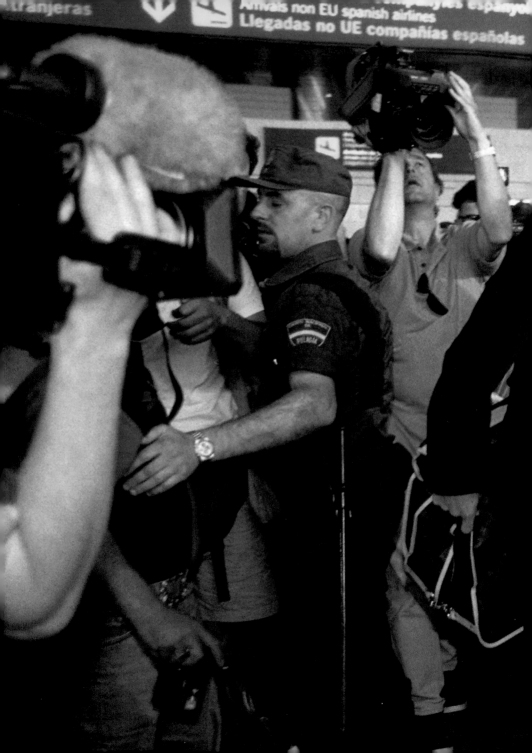

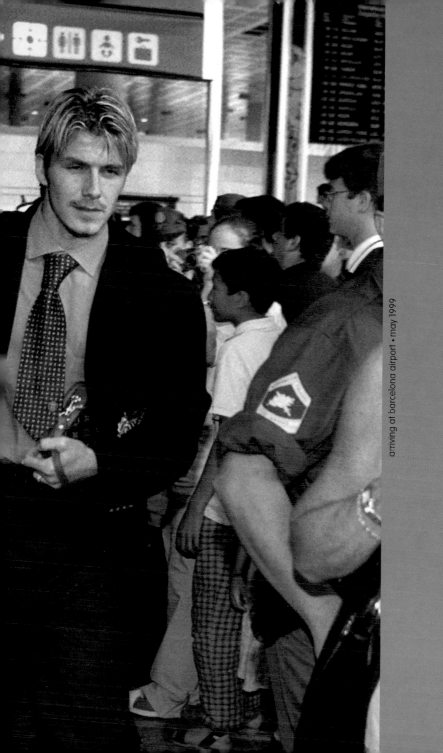

arriving at barcelona airport • may 1999

arriving at carrington training ground, manchester · february 2003

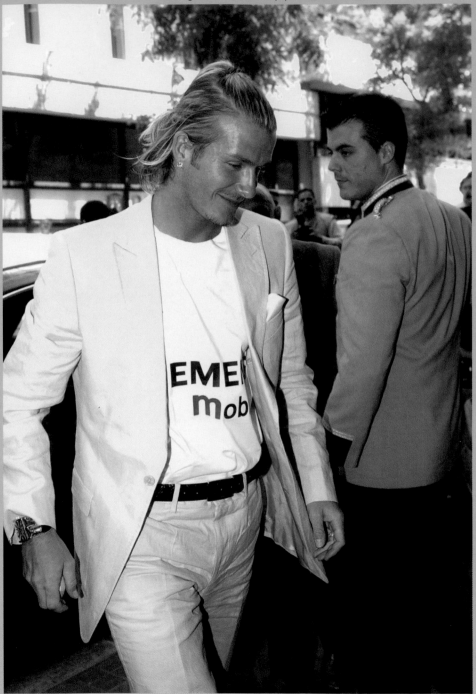

madrid • february 2004

arriving in madrid • july 2003

arriving back at the england team hotel, niigata, japan • june 2002

leaving the england team coach, london • november 2002

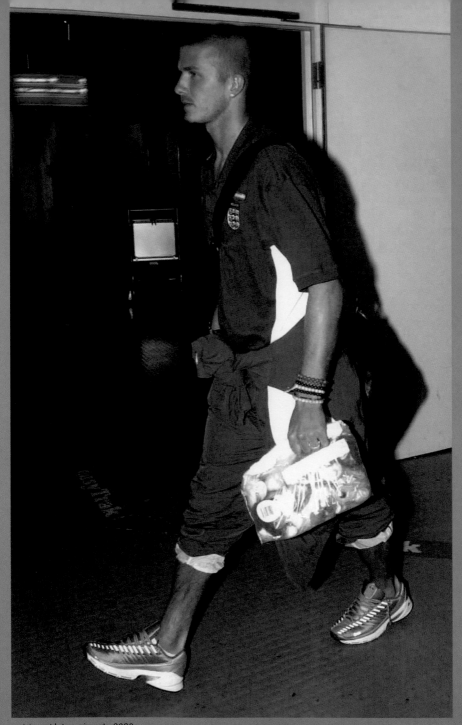

arriving at luton airport • 2000

madrid • january 2004

london • 1997

arriving at the real madrid training ground • november 2003

returning to the car at a filling station, madrid · april 2004

leaving the real madrid team coach, la coruna, spain • may 2004

manchester • august 1999

arriving before a match, southampton • october 1998

arriving at a west end show, london • june 1998

leaving the real madrid team coach, la coruna • may 2004

arriving at tokyo airport • august 2003

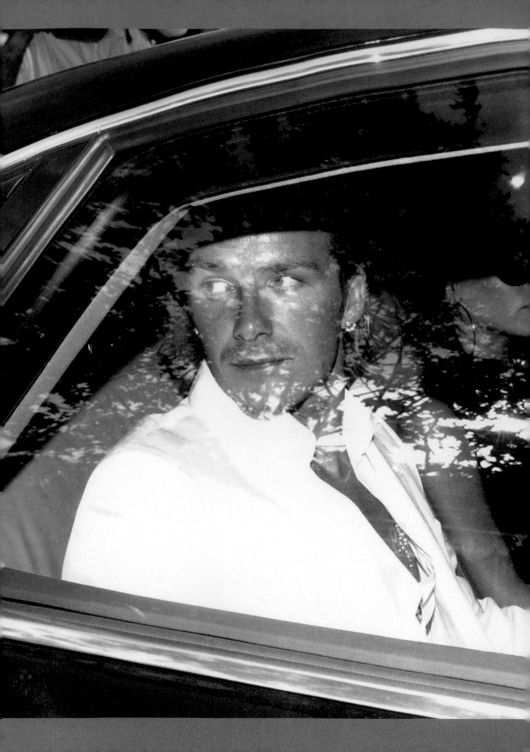

leaving training, madrid • april 2004

walking in plaza de oriente, madrid • september 2003

book signing, manchester • november 2003

leaving the hard rock café, madrid • august 2004

leaving the ivy restaurant, london • october 2003

arriving for a press conference at real madrid's training ground • november 2003

leaving a press conference at real madrid's training ground · january 2004

new york • may 2003

real madrid training ground · october 2003

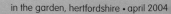

arriving at the gmex centre, manchester • march 2000

leaving claridge's hotel, london • april 2004

nice, france • july 2004

arriving at the silver clef awards, london • june 2001

arriving at the ivy restaurant, london • january 2002

arriving at simply heathcotes restaurant, manchester • august 2000

arriving at the 19 management birthday party, london • april 2004

arriving at heathrow airport • june 2003

hertfordshire • april 2003

arriving at carrington training ground, manchester • february 2003

arriving at old trafford stadium, manchester • april 200

leaving san lorenzo restaurant, london • november 2002

visiting: 10 downing street, london • may 2002

leaving the ivy restaurant, london • 1999

leaving the funeral of jimmy davis, worcestershire • august 2003

arriving at the ivy restaurant, london • march 2003

madrid · november 2003

arriving at heathrow airport • june 2003

madrid • september 2004

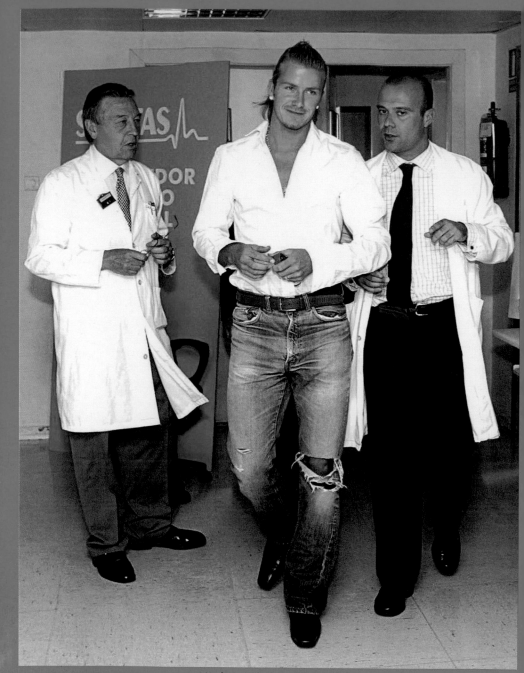

arriving for a medical, madrid • july 2003

arriving at the ivy restaurant, london • october 2003

leaving buckingham palace, london • november 2003

visiting a school, japan • 2002

leaving 10 downing street, london • october 2002

Escuela de Conducción y Seguridad Audi

racing at a track day, madrid • november 2004

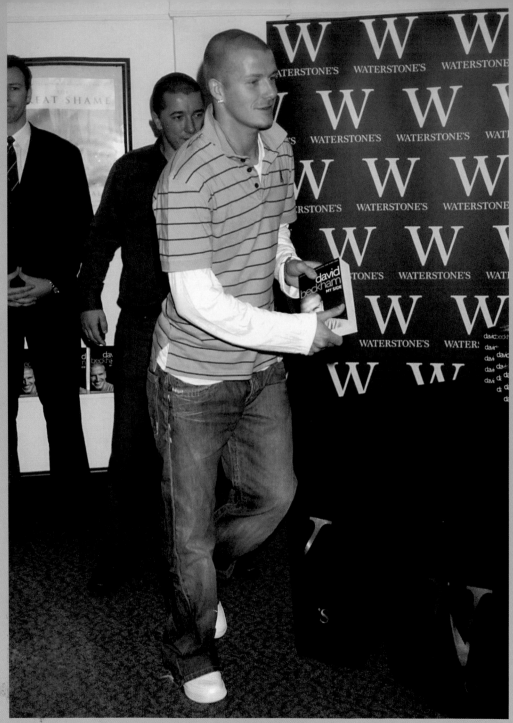

book signing, manchester • october 2004

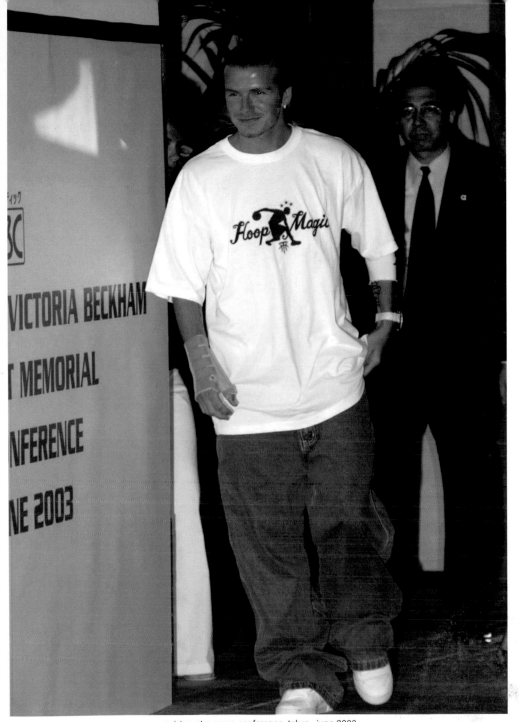

arriving at a press conference, tokyo • june 2003

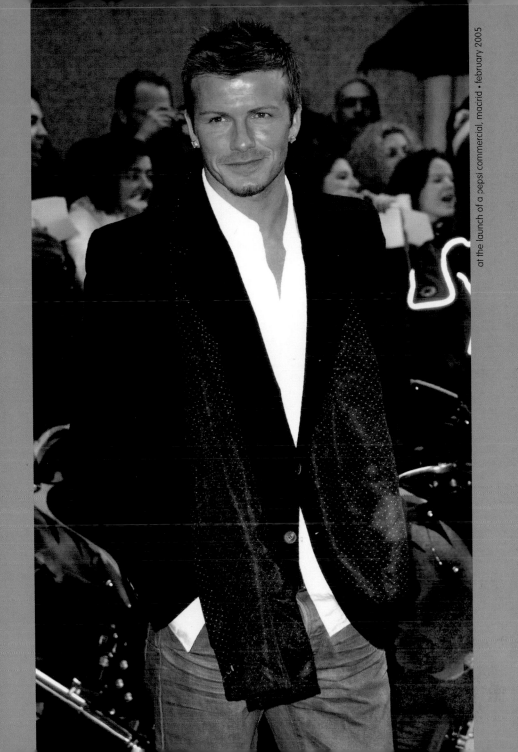

arriving in the players' box, bernebeu stadium, madrid • october 2004

arriving at the hospital de la zarzuela, madrid • july 2003

hertfordshire • july 1999

whitney houston aftershow party, london • 1999

leaving the real madrid training ground • february 2005

leaving a madrid restaurant • april 2005

leaving his house with luis figo after brooklyn's birthday party • march 2005

signing autographs and with beyoncé knowles at a pepsi commercial launch, madrid • february 2005

leaving brooklyn's birthday party, manchester • march 2003

arriving at the ruber clinic, madrid, following the birth of his third son, cruz • february 2005

a david & charles book
© david & charles 2005
first published in the uk in 2005

david & charles
brunel house, newton abbot
devon tq12 4pu
www.davidandcharles.co.uk

david & charles is an
f+w publications inc. company

a catalogue record for this book is
available from the british library

isbn 0 7153 2163 3

first published in north america
in 2005 by adams media
an f+w publications inc. company
57 littlefield street, avon, ma 02322
1-800-872-5627
www.adamsmedia.com

isbn 1-59337-515-8

printed in china by snp leefung

commissioning editor neil baber
editor jennifer proverbs
art editor mike moule
production controller kelly smith